LUCKY THIRTEEN:

Mort Cooper and the Jinx That Led to a MVP Season

By

Michael Murphy

With Selected Illustrations by Carissa McDonald

MURLOR BOOKS

Kindle Direct Publishing

Dedication

Dedicated to my father . . .

E. V. Murphy . . .

**. . . who taught me to love the
St. Louis Cardinals, first, and baseball, second.
His daily battle with arthritis taught us all the true
meaning of perseverance.**

Lucky Thirteen

In our lives we face many challenges. These challenges may include our relationships with family and friends, financial or money issues, difficulties in school or at work, and dealing with difficult people. Often these challenges stand in the way of achieving success in school or at work. Other obstacles to our success may include problems with our physical health, emotional anxieties[1], and issues with our mental well-being.

As we grow and mature as individuals, it is important to develop the character traits that help us overcome these obstacles. The challenges we face must be met with strength, courage, and perseverance[2] if we are to achieve the success we desire in our lives.

Professional athletes face many of these same difficulties and challenges in their everyday lives. But, they also face additional challenges. Overcoming injury, competition from other athletes trying to defeat them on the playing field or take their position on the team, rebounding from poor performance, or dealing with the mental aspects of their sport are all additional obstacles the professional athlete must overcome to achieve success.

Another area of life that can prove a hindrance to success is superstition. Superstition is a belief or practice that usually results from ignorance, fear of the unknown, undue trust in magic, fate, or chance, or false ideas about the causes of events. Superstitions date back to the earliest days of human life. Many superstitions have been debunked by modern science. But, others still linger in our popular culture. Among these unfounded claims are such ideas as "walking under a ladder is unlucky," or that "a black cat crossing your path brings bad luck." Others superstitions include "bad luck comes in threes" and 'picking up a penny tails down brings bad fortune."

None of these superstitions, however, are perhaps as powerful as the fear of the number 13. A quick Internet search of movies about Halloween yields a long list of films with a theme revolving around the fear of the number 13, and, of course, Friday

Belief in superstitions can pose obstacles to our success. **(Illustration by Carissa McDonald)**

the 13ᵗʰ. Hotels often do not have a thirteenth floor. Many airlines omit the 13ᵗʰ row in seating aboard airplanes. Most hospitals do not have rooms with the number 13.

Belief in these superstitions can prove to be formidable obstacles to our happiness and our success.

Superstition about the number 13 is as common-place in professional sports as it is in everyday life. Most players avoid the number fearing it will bring them the worst of all possible luck. A small minority, however, see the number in a different light. Viewing it as something of a good luck charm, these brave souls wear the number with pride.

One such man was Mort Cooper, a strapping 6'2" 210 lb. right-handed pitcher for the St. Louis Cardinals in the late 1930's and early 1940's. Cooper, after breaking in with the Cardinals in 1938 wearing uniform number 30, began

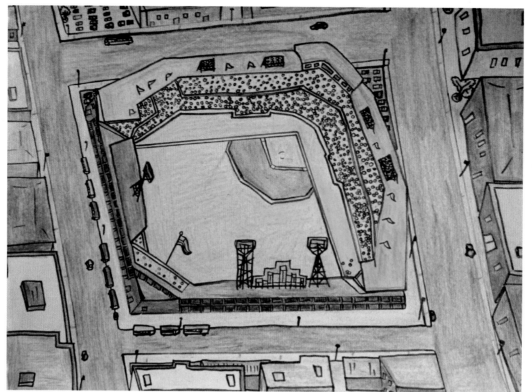

Sportsman Park-Home of the Cardinals and the St. Louis Browns in 1942. **(Illustration by Carissa McDonald)**

wearing the number 13 in 1941. Newspaper reports of the day

-Mort Cooper-(**St. Louis Cardinals 1941 Team Issue)**

described Cooper as having "thick, dark hair, a round, reddish and somewhat battered face . . . nervous, restless, and quick-tempered . . . he is a ready talker and sociable."[3]

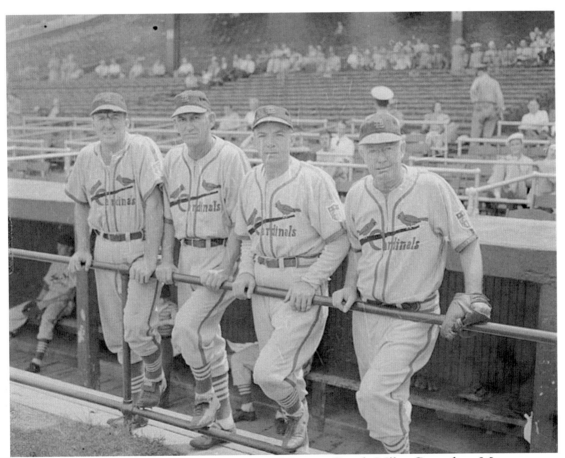

From Left: Cardinal Center Fielder Terry Moore, Coach Mike Gonzalez, Manager Billy Southworth, and Coach Buzzy Wares. **(Courtesy Boston Public Library, Leslie Jones Collection)**

Cardinal great-Stan Musial-(**Bowman Baseball Card Company**)

Cooper was known as a workhorse. Five times he threw over two hundred innings. He was also recognized by his teammates for his toughness, his perseverance, and his ability to overcome obstacles that stood in the way of success. Cardinal great Stan Musial once remarked about Cooper: "This great pitcher used to chew aspirins on the mound to dull the pain caused by bone chips in his elbow."[4]

United Press sportswriter Jack Cuddy explained Cooper's success: "Right-handed hitters get the fastball and the forkball. The latter approaches the plate in drunken fashion, like a knuckler's butterfly pitch. It's almost impossible to smack the "fork" solidly. In addition, Mort has unusual control. With a 3-and-2 count on the batsman, he can produce a feint or an actual[5] in the strike zone that forces a waiting called strike or a whiff."[6]

Brothers Walker (L) and Mort Cooper (R). (**Courtesy Boston Public Library, Leslie Jones Collection**)

In 1942, Cooper and the Cardinals were engaged in a dogfight with the Brooklyn Dodgers for the National League

Key Contributors to the 1942 Cardinals included First Baseman Johnny Hopp (L) and Outfielder Stan Musial (R). **(Courtesy Boston Public Library, Leslie Jones Collection)**

pennant. The Cardinals were managed by Billy Southworth.

Manager Billy Southworth **(St. Louis Cardinals 1941 Team Issue)**

Southworth was on his second stint as Cardinals' manager. He had first been given the job in 1929 but had been unsuccessful and was fired at mid-season and returned to the Cardinals top minor league club at Rochester, New York. Southworth had been very successful there, winning four league championships during his tenure. Cards' owner Sam Breadon had tapped him to take over the parent club again in 1940. Southworth would excel in his second stint with the club winning three consecutive pennants from 1942 through 1944 and two World Championships ('42 & '44).

Danny Litwhiler, an outfielder with the Cardinals, explained why Southworth had so much success as the Cardinals' skipper. "He was a great teacher. He taught us how to play . . . Every spring we would go through the complete fundamentals, everybody-pitchers, catchers, infielders, outfielders-all the fundamentals . . . He was a great teacher."[7]

Danny Litwhiler-(**Bowman Baseball Card Company**)

In 1942, Southworth relied upon a dominant pitching staff on his way to 106 wins as the Cardinal skipper. The staff led the National League in ERA (2.55), shutouts (18), and strikeouts (651). Anchored by Cooper and fellow starters-Johnny Beazley, Max Lanier, and Ernie White -and supplemented by a solid relief corps headed by Murray Dickson, Howie Krist and Howie Pollet the team won a Cardinal single season record 106 games. Arguably, Cooper was the ace of the staff.

Walker Cooper, Mort's brother, said of his sibling

teammate: "Mort was a shutout pitcher, a great asset anytime

and particularly in a big game when you might run into a low-

run effort yourself. Another thing, if he said he was going to

pitch a hitter one way, you could set your defense accordingly.

He wouldn't miss."[8]

Cooper's delivery-(**Play Ball Cards-Bowman Gum Company**)

Cooper was recovering from elbow surgery which he had

undergone at the conclusion of the 1941 season. The arm injury had halted Cooper's record at thirteen wins that year. In fact, despite possessing a blazing fastball, an effective slider, and a devastating forkball, Cooper had never won more than thirteen games for the Redbirds. Once he had won eleven, another time twelve, but never more than thirteen. Even in his minor league career with the Cardinals, Cooper had never won more than thirteen games. Twice he had reached this level, winning thirteen with Columbus in Double A ball in 1937 and again with Houston in the Texas League in 1938. His success in the '38 season had led to a September call-up with the Cardinals. After wearing uniform #25 during the 1940 season, Cooper had requested a uniform change to #13. He asked for the new number with the hopes that the number would "bring me above 13."[9]

Cooper & #13-(**St. Louis Cardinals 1942 Press Photo**)

But now it was August of 1942 and Cooper was sailing along with thirteen wins already to his credit. This matched his 1941 win total. With nearly two months remaining in the season, it appeared his comeback from surgery was complete. It also seemed he was poised to finally achieve the promise he had always possessed. A twenty win season was within his grasp.

Stan Musial, who was playing his first full season in St, Louis, had once said of Cooper that he "had a very good fastball and good fork ball. He didn't walk anybody. It was a pleasure to play behind him because he knew where he was going to pitch the hitters and you could play them accordingly, confident of Cooper's control."[10] Cooper seemed destined for a magical season.

But then bad luck struck again! Twice Cooper went to the mound to claim his fourteenth win and twice he failed. Thirteen! What had once been a good luck charm to Cooper now appeared to be a jinx. The spell the number held over his career had to be broken.

In desperation Cooper hit upon a scheme. His next starting assignment was against Cincinnati and when it came time for him to warm up he strolled to the mound stuffed into uniform number fourteen. That jersey had belonged to the 5'10" 185 lb. Gus Mancuso, a back-up catcher for the Cards. The number hadn't been reassigned since Mancuso's trade to the New York Giants in early May. Despite the uniform's snugness, the "magic" worked. Cooper tossed a complete-game, two hit

Gus Mancuso-(**St. Louis Cardinals 1941 Team Issue**)

shutout against the Reds winning 4-0. It was Cooper's

fourteenth win of the season.

The scheme had worked once, and Cooper, being just a

little superstitious, had to try it again. The next time he

pitched, he faced Chicago wearing uniform number fifteen,

which belonged to his brother, Cardinal catcher Walker

Cooper. Once again the "magic" worked as Mort beat the

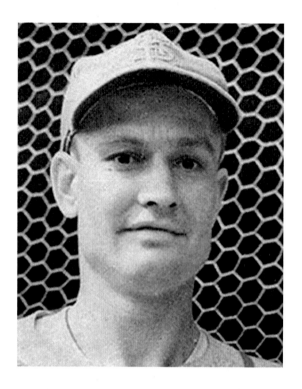

Mort's brother –Walker Cooper-**(St. Louis Cardinals 1941 Team Issue)**

Cubs 5-1. The "jinx" had truly been broken.

Cooper's next appearance was in relief. Pitching two innings against the Pirates, he suffered the lost, his seventh of the season. It was the last game Cooper would lose during the 1942 regular season. Wearing a different uniform number during his next seven starts, Cooper won each time. His last three wins were all by shutout defeating Brooklyn 3-0, Chicago 1-0, and Cincinnati 6-0.

Exchanging uniform numbers. **(Illustration by Carissa McDonald)**

Altogether, it was a tremendous season. Cooper went 22-7 and led the league not only in wins with his 22, but in ERA (1.78), shutouts (10), WHIP (0.987),[11] and fewest hits per nine innings pitched (6.7). He also finished among the leaders in 10 other pitching categories. His "Wins Above Replacement"[12] rating was 8.4.[13] More importantly, his ace pitching had led the Cardinals to the National League pennant, edging out the Brooklyn Dodgers by a razor thin margin of two games.

As the season drew to a close, speculation about the Most Valuable Player award began to center on Cooper. There were

MOST VALUABLE

PLAYER AWARD

several top candidates for the award including three of

Enos Slaughter-**(Bowman Baseball Card Company)**

Cooper's Cardinal teammates. The strongest challenge to

Cooper came from Cardinal right-fielder Enos Slaughter who

had hit 13 home runs, recorded 98 RBI, and hit .318. He had

Slaughter's hitting form-**(St. Louis Cardinals 1941 Team Issue)**

also tallied 188 hits, scored 100 runs, and had an OPS[14] of .412 and a slugging percentage[15] of .494.[16] Nicknamed "Country," Slaughter was known for his hustle and hard play. Arthur Daley, Pulitzer Prize winning sportswriter for the *New York Times*, commented about Slaughter's actions on the diamond: "On the ball field he is perpetual motion itself… He would run through a brick wall, if necessary, to make a catch, or slide into a pit of ground glass to score a run."[17] Slaughter's teammate, Stan Musial, echoed these same sentiments when he said of Slaughter, "Enos Slaughter was a tough competitor. He came to play. When he put his uniform on, you knew he was out to beat you. He was one of the great hustlers of baseball. He loved baseball. He always ran hard and played hard."[18] That hustle had now made Slaughter one of the most serious contenders for MVP honors in 1942.

Marty Marion-**(St. Louis Cardinals 1941 Team Issue)**

A second Cardinal challenger was shortstop Marty
Marion. Marion's stellar defense-he finished in the top three in
five defensive categories including assists, putouts, double
plays, fielding percentage and Defensive WAR-made him a
leading candidate. He had also led the league in doubles with
38 while batting .276. [19] Manager Billy Southworth had high
praise for Marion, "Maybe I'm prejudiced because I see him
every day, but he's the best ever. Yes, he's Mr. Shortstop in
person. He anticipates plays perfectly, can go to his right or
left equally well and has a truly great arm. Some of the things

he does have to be seen to be believed."[20] Boston Braves skipper, the legendary Casey Stengel, said of Marion, "He robbed us of base hits all day long, and I swear on one play he had three extra arms. The guy's uncanny. All he has to do is throw his glove on the diamond and (Cardinals owner Sam) Breadon's got an infield."[21] Marion's defensive prowess would earn him many votes for MVP.

Fellow starting pitcher Johnny Beazley was the third Cardinal candidate for the award. In 1941, following a standout minor league season in New Orleans, Beazley had started the Cardinals final regular season game against the Chicago Cubs. Scattering 10 hits in a complete game 3-1 win, Beazley's gutsy performance had impressed Cards' manager Billy Southworth. In 1942, Southworth gave Beazley a chance to make the big league roster. Beginning the season in the bullpen, Johnny had several successful outings. This resulted in a move into the starting rotation were Beazley excelled.[22]

Ernie Bonham (left) and Johnny Beazley before Game 2 of the 1942 World Series.
(Courtesy of Tennessee State Library and Archives)

Beazley had finished the season with a 21-6 won-lost record, pitched over 215 innings, and posted an ERA of 2.13.[23] He had also won two key games in the season's final week, posting complete game victories over Cincinnati (4-2) on September 23rd and Chicago (4-1) four days later on the 27th. [24]

Mel Ott-**(Goudey Gum Company)**

Other viable contenders for the award included New York Giant teammates Mel Ott and Johnny Mize. Ott, one of the game's most feared sluggers, had been named the Giants player-manager to begin the 1942 season. He had led the team to a third place finish behind the Cardinals and the Dodgers. In addition to his managerial duties, Ott had hit 30 home runs with 93 RBI while batting .295 with an OPS of .415 and a slugging percentage of .497. He had led the league in home runs with his 30, in walks with 109, and in runs scored with 118. [25] Extremely popular with Giant fans, Ott had a reputation as one of the game's great gentlemen. A writer in *The Sporting News* had described him as "a quiet, modest hero" and had stated that his "gentleness, kindness and good sportsmanship always set a fine example."[26]

Johnny Mize-**(Baseball Digest-March 1948)**

Mize, the former Cardinal first baseman in his first season with the Giants following his trade from the Redbirds, had similar numbers to Ott's. Mize had batted .305 with 26 homers and 110 RBI. He had finished the season with an OPS of .380 and a slugging percentage of .521.[27] He had topped the league in both RBI and slugging percentage. Nicknamed "The Big Cat," Mize was known for his compact swing. Casey Stengel described his stroke: "His bat doesn't travel as far as anybody else's. He just cocks it and slaps, and when you're as big as he is, you can slap a ball into the seats. That short swing is wonderful."[28]

-Mize is the only player to hit 50 home runs in a season and strike out less than 50 times. A feat he achieved in 1947. **(St. Louis Cardinals Team Issue-1941)**

Mickey Owen-**(Bowman Baseball Card Company)**

A trio of Dodger players were also top contenders for MVP. Mickey Owen, the Dodger catcher and also a former Cardinal, had masterfully handled the Brooklyn pitching staff. Dodger pitchers had finished among the league leaders in nine major pitching categories including ERA (2.84), shutouts (15), innings pitched (1398.2), strikeouts (612), and saves (24). Owen had hit .259 and posted a fielding percentage of .987 over 133 games.[29]

Pete Reiser-**(Bowman Baseball Card Company)**

Owen's teammate, and former Cardinal farmhand, Pete Reiser was another solid MVP candidate. Reiser had hit .310 with 149 hits and a league leading 20 stolen bases.[30] He had also played stellar center field defense. Reiser, whose career would be cut short by devastating injuries, received high praise in the 1976 book *Nice Guys Finish Last* written by his Dodger manager, Leo Durocher. Durocher had written: "There will never be a ballplayer as good as Willie Mays, but (Pete) Reiser was every bit as good and he might have been better. Pete Reiser might have been the best ballplayer I ever saw. He had more power than Willie. He could throw as good as Willie.

Mays was fast, but Reiser was faster. Name whoever you want to, and Pete Reiser was faster. Willie Mays had everything. Pete Reiser had everything but luck."[31] These talents, amply displayed in 1942, had made Reiser a leading MVP candidate.

Dolph Camilli-**(Goudey Gum Company)**

Brooklyn first baseman, Dolph Camilli, was the final Dodger candidate. Camilli was looking to repeat as the league's MVP having won the award in 1941 over his Dodger teammates Reiser and Whit Wyatt. Camilli had amassed 300 points to win the award that season garnering nineteen first place votes.[32] Now only one season removed from the end of his 12-year big league career, Camilli, in 1942, had hit 26 home runs, driven home 109 and hit .252. His slugging percentage was .471[33]

Rounding out the group of potential MVP's were Bob Elliott of the Pittsburgh Pirates and Claude Passeau of the Chicago Cubs. Elliot, the Pirate third baseman, had hit .296 with 9 home runs and 89 RBI. He had finished third in the league in hits with 166. Elliott's play in the field was also impressive having led all NL third basemen in putouts (173) and assists (285) while posting a fielding percentage of .927.[34]

-Bob Elliott (**Bowman Gum Company**)

Passeau, a workhorse right-handed starter for the Chicago Cubs, had posted a 19-14 record in an All-Star season. His ERA had been 2.68 with 3 shutouts and 24 complete games in 34 starts.[35] Pitching for a Cubs team that would finish in 6th place 38 games behind the pennant winning Cardinals, Passeau had proven his value. Joe King, a sports writer for the *New York World Telegram* had remarked about Passeau's outstanding season: "It's a pity Claude Passeau is working for a club so lowly as the Cubs. For service to his team Passeau isn't surpassed by anyone — he holds the pitching staff together."[36]

Despite these strong contenders for the award, Cooper had several intangible factors that might work in his favor with the award voters. Foremost among those factors was the perseverance and tenacity he had displayed in overcoming the elbow injury which had hindered his 1941 season. Also his ingenuity in overcoming the "13 jinx" might appeal to the baseball writers.

Since 1931 the MVP Award had been issued annually by the Baseball Writers Association of America. In 1942, the MVP was determined by a vote of three writers from each baseball city. Each writer submitted a 10-player ballot. Players were awarded 14 points for a 1st place vote, 9 points for a 2nd, 8 points for a 3rd position vote and so on down to 1 point for a 10th place vote. As was usual in most MVP voting, the number of 1st place votes was crucial in determining the ultimate winner of the award. 1942 would be no different. However, what would be uncanny about that vote would be the *number* of 1st place votes the winner would receive.

The results of the MVP voting were released in late October. A headline in *The Sporting News*, the bible of baseball, proclaimed the outcome in poetic rhyme: **"SUPER DOOPER COOPER:** Card Pitching Ace Most Valuable Player in N.L."[37] A secondary headline detailed Cooper's reaction: "'You Deserved It'" Snapped Dad as Mort Blushed

Over Honor."[38] Cooper had won the prestigious award!! He had outdistanced his nearest MVP competitor, teammate Enos Slaughter, with 263 points compared to Slaughter's 200. Cooper had captured the prize by garnering more first place votes than any of his rivals. One can just imagine the surprise with which Cooper greeted the news that of the twenty-four first place votes cast, he had received the unbelievable number of THIRTEEN![39] In a career that had once appeared to have been jinxed by the number 13, Cooper discovered that the number was truly magical for him. Cooper's perseverance and tenacity in overcoming injury and superstition had earned him the highest honor his sport had to offer.

Unfortunately, the perseverance that had marked Cooper's baseball career was not translated to his personal life. After several more successful seasons with the Cardinals his personal troubles began to take a toll on his career. Cooper's first marriage had ended tragically in 1936 when his first wife, Mary, died in a car accident. By 1945, his second marriage to

Bernadine Owen, had fallen apart and their divorce would be played out in newspaper headlines across the country.[40]

In addition to marital troubles, Cooper had angered Cardinal owner Sam Breadon with a short-lived salary holdout at the beginning of the 1945 season.[41] In May, he was traded to the Boston Braves where he re-injured his elbow. His career was over by 1949.[42]

More personal troubles would follow. Bad business investments, mounting debts, and a struggle with substance abuse marked his final years. Hospitalized with liver disease, pneumonia, and diabetes, he died in 1958. He was only 45 years old.[43]

Perseverance, tenacity, and ingenuity had marked Cooper's career with the Cardinals. These character traits had been fully evident in the summer of 1942. Twice more during his career he would win twenty games for the Cardinals (21 in 1943 and 22 in 1944), but never again did he have a season like the one in 1942: The summer of his "Lucky Thirteen."

13

The MVP Vote (Top Ten):[44]

	Player	Team	Total	1st Place	%
1	Mort Cooper	STL	263.0	13.0	78%
2	Enos Slaughter	STL	200.0	6.0	60%
3	Mel Ott	NYG	190.0	4.0	57%
4	Mickey Owen	BRO	103.0	0.0	31%
5	Johnny Mize	NYG	97.0	0.0	29%
6	Pete Reiser	BRO	91.0	0.0	27%
7	Marty Marion	STL	81.0	1.0	24%
8	Dolph Camilli	BRO	42.0	0.0	13%
9	Bob Elliott	PIT	39.0	0.0	12%
10	Claude Passeau	CHC	33.0	0.0	10%

The Uniform Changes[45]

#	Player
14	Gus Mancuso
15	Walker Cooper
16	Ken O'Dea
17	Erv Dusak
18	Lon Warneke
19	Harry Gumbert
20	Coaker Triplett
21	Johnny Beazley
22	Murray Dickson

Mort Cooper's Career Statistics[46]

Year	Team	W	L	G	GS	CG	SHO	SV	IP	H	R	ER	ERA	WHIP	HR	BB	SO	IBB	WP	HBP	BK	WAR
1938	SLC	2	1	4	3	1	0	1	23.2	17	11	8	3.04	1.23	1	12	11	0	0	1	0	0.3
1939	SLC	12	6	45	26	7	2	4	210.2	208	94	76	3.25	1.45	6	97	130	0	4	2	1	3.2
1940	SLC	11	12	38	29	16	3	3	230.2	225	103	93	3.63	1.35	12	86	95	0	5	3	2	4.0
1941	SLC	13	9	29	25	12	0	0	186.2	175	88	81	3.91	1.31	15	69	118	0	7	3	0	1.3
1942	SLC	22	7	37	35	22	10	0	278.2	207	73	55	1.78	0.99	9	68	152	0	5	5	0	8.4
1943	SLC	21	8	37	32	24	6	3	274.0	228	81	70	2.30	1.12	5	79	141	0	4	5	2	5.8
1944	SLC	22	7	34	33	22	7	1	252.1	227	74	69	2.46	1.14	6	60	97	0	0	5	1	5.3
1945	SLC	2	0	4	3	1	0	0	23.2	20	7	4	1.52	1.14	1	7	14	0	0	1	0	0.6
1945	BOS	7	4	20	11	4	1	1	78.0	77	35	29	3.35	1.33	4	27	45	0	0	1	0	0.7
1946	BOS	13	11	28	27	15	4	1	199.0	181	76	69	3.12	1.11	16	39	83	0	2	0	1	3.4
1947	BOS	2	5	10	7	2	0	0	46.2	48	26	21	4.05	1.31	2	13	15	0	0	2	0	0.1
1947	NYG	1	5	8	8	2	0	0	36.2	51	32	29	7.12	1.75	7	13	12	0	0	0	0	-0.9
1949	CHI	0	0	1	0	0	0	0	0.0	2	3	3	0.00	0.00	1	1	0	0	1	0	0	xx
Career		128	75	295	239	128	33	14	1840.2	1666	703	607	2.97	1.22	85	571	913	0	28	28	7	xx

Mort Cooper's World Series Pitching Statistics

Year	Team	W	L	G	GS	CG	SHO	SV	IP	H	R	ER	ERA	WHIP	HR	BB	SO	IBB	WP	HBP	BK
1942	WS SLC	0	1	2	2	0	0	0	13.0	17	10	8	5.54	1.62	1	4	9	0	0	0	0
1943	WS SLC	1	1	2	2	1	0	0	16.0	11	5	5	2.81	0.88	1	3	10	0	1	0	0
1944	WS SLC	1	1	2	2	1	1	0	16.0	9	2	2	1.13	0.88	1	5	16	0	0	0	0
		2	3	6	6	2	1	0	45.0	37	17	15	3.00	1.09	3	12	35	0	1	0	0

Photo Credits

Front Cover- St. Louis Cardinals – 1942 Press Photo. (Photo in the Public Domain and available at Wikipedia.org.)

Page 6-Illustration by Carissa McDonald

Page 8- (top)-Illustration by Carissa McDonald

Page 8 (bottom) - St. Louis Cardinals - 1941 Team Issue (Photo in the Public Domain and available at Wikipedia.org.)

Page 9 - Courtesy of the Boston Public Library, Leslie Jones Collection.

Page 10-Bowman Baseball Card Company. (Photo in the Public Domain and available at Wikipedia.org.)

Page 11- Courtesy of the Boston Public Library, Leslie Jones Collection.

Page 12- (top) Courtesy of the Boston Public Library, Leslie Jones Collection.

Page 12- (bottom) St. Louis Cardinals – 1941 Team Issue. (Photo in the Public Domain and available at Wikipedia.org.)

Page 14- Bowman Baseball Card Company. (Photo in the Public Domain and available at Wikipedia.org.)

Page 15-Play Ball Cards-Bowman Gum Company. (Photo in the Public Domain and available at Wikipedia.org.)

Page 17- St. Louis Cardinals – 1942 Press Photo. (Photo in the Public Domain and available at Wikipedia.org.)

Page 19- St. Louis Cardinals-1941 Team Issue. (Photo in the Public Domain and available at Wikipedia.org.)

Page 20- St. Louis Cardinals-1941 Team Issue. (Photo in the Public Domain and available at Wikipedia.org.)
Page 21- Illustration by Carissa McDonald
Page 23 (top)-Bowman Baseball Card Company. (Photo in the Public Domain and available at Wikipedia.org.)
Page 23 (bottom)-St. Louis Cardinals-1941 Team Issue. (Photo in the Public Domain and available at Wikipedia.org.)
Page 25- St. Louis Cardinals-1941 Team Issue. (Photo in the Public Domain and available at Wikipedia.org.)
Page 27- Courtesy Tennessee State Library and Archives
Page 28- Goudey Gum Company. (Photo in the Public Domain and available at Wikipedia.org.)
Page 29- Baseball Digest, March 1948. (Photo in the Public Domain and available at Wikipedia.org.)
Page 30-St. Louis Cardinals Team Issue-1941. (Photo in the Public Domain and available at Wikipedia.org.
Page 31- Bowman Baseball Card Company. (Photo in the Public Domain and available at Wikipedia.org.)
Page 32- Bowman Baseball Card Company. (Photo in the Public Domain and available at Wikipedia.org.)
Page 33 - Goudey Gum Company. (Photo in the Public Domain and available at Wikipedia.org.)
Page 34 – Bowman Gum Company. (Photo in the Public Domain and available at Wikipedia.org.)
Page 52-Illustration by Carissa McDonald
Back Cover Author Photo-Swafford Photography, Bernie, Missouri

Bibliography

Baseball Almanac. "Mort Cooper Stats." Copyright 2000-2018. Baseball-Almanac, Inc. Available at: http://www.baseball-almanac.com/players/player.php?p=coopemo01.

Baseball Almanac. "1942 St. Louis Cardinals Roster." Baseball Almanac, Inc. Copyright 2000-2018.
Available at:
www.baseballalmanac.com/teamstats/roster.php?y=1942&t=SLN.

Baseball Reference. Gracenote: A Nielsen Company. Copyright 2000-2019. Sports Reference, LLC.

Broeg, Bob. The Man: Stan Musial, Then and Now. St. Louis: The Bethany Press, 1977.

Claerbaut, David. Cardinals Essential: Everything You Need To Know To Be A Real Fan. Chicago: Triumph Books, 2006.

Cohen, Robert W. The 50 Greatest Players in St. Louis Cardinals History. Boulder, CO: Taylor Trade Publishing, 2015.

"Cooper Brothers Holding Out For $15,000 in 1945." Lawrence Journal World. Associated Press. April 16, 1945, p. 6.

Durocher, Leo with Ed Linn. Nice Guys Finish Last. New York: Simon and Schuster, 1975.

"Enos Slaughter." National Baseball Hall of Fame: Biographies. Cooperstown, New York. Available at baseballhall.org › Hall of Famers.

Fuqua, John. "Johnny Beazley." Society for American Baseball Research. Available at https://sabr.org/bioproj/person/82e225d5. Accessed 5 April 2019.

Godar, Ben. "The End of the Greatest Cardinals Pitching Staff." 4 September 2015. SBNATION: Retro Birdos. Vox Media, 2018.

Golenbock, Peter. The Spirit of St. Louis: A History of the St. Louis Cardinals and Browns. New York: Avon Books, Inc., 2000.

Grabowski, John. Baseball Legends: Stan Musial. New York: Chelsea House Publishers, 1993.

King, Joe, "Ott Candidate For Best Player Award," *New York World- Telegram*, August 17, 1942.

"Marty Marion." National Baseball Hall of Fame: Biographies. Cooperstown, New York. Available at baseballhall.org › Hall of Famers.

"Mel Ott Left a Legacy as a Classy Player and Person." RetroSimba. November 21, 2018. Available at https://retrosimba.com/2018/11/21/mel-ott-left-a-legacy-as-a .. Accessed 6 April 2019.

Merriam-Webster. "Anxiety." Merriam-Webster 2019. Available at: https://merrian-webster.com/dictionary/anxiety.

Merriam-Webster. "Perseverance." Merriam-Webster 2019. Available at: https://merrian-webster.com/dictionary/perseverance.

"Mort Cooper." Everipedia International. 2018.

"Mort Cooper." The Baseball Nexus. Tramant, LLC.

"Mort Cooper." Wikipedia, the Free Encyclopedia. 21 August 2018.

"Mort Cooper, Former Cardinal Hurler, Dies." The Nevada Daily Mail. November 14, 1958.

"Mort Cooper Released." Pittsburgh Post Gazette. May 10, 1949, p. 14.

"Mort Cooper's Wife Will Divorce Pitcher." St. Petersburg Times. November 8, 1945, p. 12.

"Online slang dictionary, language guide to speak Baseball Slang." Available at: www.aboutlanguageschools.com/slang/baseball-slang.asp.

Neuman, Jeffrey and John Warner Davenport. The Cardinals. New York: Macmillan Publishing Company, Inc., 1983.

Rains, Bob The St. Louis Cardinals: The 100th Anniversary History. New York: St. Martin's Press, 1992.

Ross, Alan. Cardinals Glory: for the Love of Dizzy, Ozzie, and the Man. Nashville: Cumberland House, 2005.

Schoor, Gene. The Stan Musial Story. New York: Julian Messner, Inc., 1955.

"Slugging Percentage (SLG)." MLB Advanced Media, LP. May 24, 2018. Available at: http://m.mlb.com/glossary/standard-stats/slugging-percentage.

Stewart, Wayne. Stan the Man: The Life and Times of Stan Musial. Chicago: Triumph Books, 2010.

The Sporting News. October 29, 1942.

Tomasik, Mark. RetroSimba. "How Mort Cooper Pitched 2 Straight 1-Hitters for the Cards." June 22, 2012. Blog at World Press.com. Available at https://retrosimba.com.

Vecsey, George. Stan Musial: An American Life. New York: Ballantine Books, 2011.

"What is OPS in Baseball? Quora. Available at: https://www.Quora.com/What-is-OPS-in-Baseball.

Wolf, Gregory H. "Mort Cooper." Society for American Baseball Research. Available at: https://sabr.org/bioproj/person/9c707ace.

Endnotes

---

[1] Anxiety is defined as an abnormal and overwhelming sense of apprehension and fear often marked by physical signs (such as tension, sweating, and increased pulse rate), by doubt concerning the reality and nature of the threat, and by self-doubt about one's capacity to cope with it. See Merriam-Webster. "Anxiety." Merriam-Webster 2019. Available at: https://merrian-webster.com/dictionary/anxiety. Accessed 5 February 2019.

[2] Perseverance is defined as a continued effort to do or achieve something despite difficulties, failure, or opposition. See Merriam-Webster. "Perseverance." Merriam-Webster 2019. Available at: https://merrian-webster.com/dictionary/perseverance. Accessed 4 February 2019.

[3] Bob Rains. The St. Louis Cardinals: The 100th Anniversary History. New York: St. Martin's Press, 1992. p. 102.

[4] Baseball Almanac. "Mort Cooper Stats." Copyright 2000-2018. Baseball-Almanac, Inc. Available at: http://www.baseball-almanac.com/players/player.php?p=coopemo01. Accessed 2 October 2018.

5 An "actual" was a nickname for any pitch intended to establish a pitcher's command of the inside portion of the strike zone, usually involving throwing a pitch at or near a hitter who may be covering that portion of the strike zone. Online slang dictionary, language guide to speak Baseball Slang. Available at:www.aboutlanguageschools.com/slang/baseball-slang.asp. Accessed 5 June 2019.

[6] Mark Tomasik. RetroSimba. "How Mort Cooper Pitched 2 Straight 1-Hitters for the Cards." June 22, 2012. Blog at World Press.com Available at https://retrosimba.com. Access 28 August 2018. (Original quote attributed to Jack Cuddy of United Press).

[7] Peter Golenbock. The Spirit of St. Louis: A History of the St. Louis Cardinals and Browns. New York: Avon Books, Inc. p. 254.

[8] Rains, op. cit., p. 103.

[9] Ibid, p. 95.

[10] Baseball Almanac. "Mort Cooper Stats." Copyright 2000-2018. Baseball-Almanac, Inc. Available at: http://www.baseball-almanac.com/players/player.php?p=coopemo01. Accessed 2 October 2018.

[11] WHIP is defined as the number of walks and hits allowed per 9 innings pitched.

[12] WAR-Wins Above Replacement is a sabermetric statistic calculated to be the number of additional wins that player's team has achieved above the number of expected team wins if that player were substituted with a replacement-level player. See "Wins Above Replacement." Wikipedia: The Free Encyclopedia. 31 October 2018; "What is WAR?" FanGraphs Sabermetrics Library Available at: https://www.fangraphs.com/library/misc/war/1 . Updated 3 Dec 2018.; and

Baseball-Reference.com WAR Explained. Baseball-Reference.com *https://www.baseball-reference.com/about/war_explained.shtml.* Gracenote: A Nielsen Company 2010-2018. All accessed 5 December 2018.

[13] Baseball Reference. "Mort Cooper." Gracenote: A Nielsen Company. Copyright 2000-2018. Sports Reference, LLC. Available at: https://baseball-reference.com/players/c/cooper Accessed 23 September 2018.

[14] An OPS is a hitter's on base percentage plus his slugging percentage (see endnote #15). "What is OPS in Baseball? Quora. Available at: https://www.Quora.com/What-is-OPS-in baseball. Accessed 4 December 2018.

[15] Slugging percentage is the total number of bases a player records per at-bat. Unlike on-base percentage, slugging percentage calculates only hits and does not include walks and being hit by a pitch. The formula for slugging percentage is: $(1B + 2Bx2 + 3Bx3 + HRx4)/AB$. See "Slugging Percentage (SLG)." MLB Advanced Media, LP. May 24, 2018. Available at: http://m.mlb.com/glossary/standard-stats/slugging-percentage.

[16] Baseball Reference. "Enos Slaughter." Gracenote: A Nielsen Company. Copyright 2000-2018. Sports Reference, LLC. Available at: https://www.baseball-reference.com/players/s/slaugen01.shtml. Accessed 1 October 2018.

[17] "Enos Slaughter." National Baseball Hall of Fame: Biographies. Cooperstown, New York. Available at **baseballhall.org** › Hall of Famers. Accessed 2 April 2019.

[18] Robert W. Cohen. The 50 Greatest Players in St. Louis Cardinals History. Boulder, CO: Taylor Trade Publishing, 2015. p. 94.

[19] Baseball Reference. "Marty Marion" Gracenote: A Nielsen Company. Copyright 2000-2018. Sports Reference, LLC. Available at: https://www.baseball-reference.com/players/m/marioma01.shtml. Accessed 30 September 2018.

[20] "Marty Marion." National Baseball Hall of Fame: Biographies. Cooperstown, New York. Available at **baseballhall.org** › Hall of Famers. Accessed 3 April 2019.

[21] Ibid.

[22] John Fuqua. "Johnny Beazley." Society for American Baseball Research. Available at https://sabr.org/bioproj/person/82e225d5. Accessed 5 April 2019.

[23] Baseball Reference. "Johnny Beazley." Gracenote: A Nielsen Company. Copyright 2000-2018. Sports Reference, LLC. Available at: https://www.baseball-reference.com/players/b/beazljo01.shtml, Accessed 1 October 2018.

[24] Baseball Reference. "St. Louis Cardinals 1942 Schedule." Gracenote: A Nielsen Company. Copyright 2000-2018. Sports Reference, LLC. Available at: https://www.baseballl reference.com/teams/STL/1942-schedule-scores.shtml. Accessed 2 October 2018.

[25] Baseball Reference. "Mel Ott." Gracenote: A Nielsen Company. Copyright 2000-2018. Sports Reference, LLC. Available at: https://www.baseball-reference.com/players/o/ottme01.shtml. Accessed 29 September 2018.

[26] "Mel Ott Left a Legacy as a Classy Player and Person." RetroSimba. November 21, 2018. Available at https://retrosimba.com/2018/11/21/mel-ott-left-a-legacy-as-a .. Accessed 6 April 2019.

[27] Baseball Reference. "Johnny Mize." Gracenote: A Nielsen Company. Copyright 2000-2018. Sports Reference, LLC. Available at: https://www.baseball-reference.com/players/m/mizejo01.shtml. Accessed 29 September 2018.

[28] Baseball Reference. "Johnny Mize: BR Bullpen." Gracenote: A Nielsen Company. Copyright 2000-2019. Sports Reference, LLC. Available at: https://www.baseball-reference.com/bullpen/Johnny_Mize. Accessed 7 April 2019.

[29] Baseball Reference. "Mickey Owen." Gracenote: A Nielsen Company. Copyright 2000-2018. Sports Reference, LLC. Available at: https://www.baseball-reference.com/players/o/owenmi.01.shtml. Accessed 27 September 2018.

[30] Baseball Reference. "Dolph Camilli." Gracenote: A Nielsen Company. Copyright 2000-2018. Sports Reference, LLC. Available at: https://www.baseball-reference.com/players/r/reisepe01.shtml. Accessed 29 September 2018.

[31] Leo Durocher with Ed Linn. Nice Guys Finish Last. New York: Simon and Schuster, 1975. p. 431.

[32] Baseball Reference. "1941 Awards Voting." Gracenote: A Nielsen Company. Copyright 2000-2018. Sports Reference, LLC. Available at: https://www.baseballreference.com/awards/awards_1941.shtml. Accessed 6 April 2019.

[33] Baseball Reference. "Dolph Camilli." Gracenote: A Nielsen Company. Copyright 2000-2018. Sports Reference, LLC. Available at: https://www.baseball-reference.com/players/c/camildo01.shtml. Accessed 27 September 2018.

[34] Baseball Reference. "Bob Elliott." Gracenote: A Nielsen Company. Copyright 2000-2019. Sports Reference, LLC. Available at: https://www.baseball-reference.com/players/e/elliobo01.shtml. Accessed 7 July 2019.

[35] Baseball Reference. "Claude Passeau." Gracenote: A Nielsen Company. Copyright 2000-2019. Sports Reference, LLC. Available at: https://www.baseball-reference.com/players/p/passecl01.shtml Accessed 7 July 2019.

[36] Joe King, "Ott Candidate For Best Player Award," New York World- Telegram, August 17, 1942.

[37] The Sporting News. October 29, 1942, p.1.

[38] Ibid.

[39] Baseball Reference. "1942 Awards Voting." Gracenote: A Nielsen Company. Copyright 2000-2018. Sports Reference, LLC. Available at: https://www.baseballreference.com/awards/awards_1942.shtml. Accessed 5 October 2018.

[40] "Mort Cooper's Wife Will Divorce Pitcher." St. Petersburg Times. November 8, 1945, p. 12.

[41] "Cooper Brothers Holding Out For $15,000 in 1945." <u>Lawrence Journal World</u>. Associated Press. April 16, 1945, p. 6.

[42] "Mort Cooper Released." <u>Pittsburgh Post Gazette</u>. May 10, 1949, p. 14.

[43] "Mort Cooper, Former Cardinal Hurler, Dies." <u>The Nevada Daily Mail</u>. November 14, 1958.

[44] Baseball Reference. "1942 Awards Voting." Gracenote: A Nielsen Company. Copyright 2000-2018. Sports Reference, LLC. Available at: <u>https://www.baseballreference.com/awards/awards_1942.shtml</u>. Accessed 5 October 2018.

[45] Baseball Almanac. "1942 St. Louis Cardinals Roster." Baseball Almanac, Inc. Copyright 2000-2018. Available at: <u>www.baseball-almanac.com/teamstats/roster.php?y=1942&t=SLN</u>. Accessed 3 December 3, 2018.

[46] Mort Cooper's career statistics were complied and verified from a number of sources. These included: "Mort Cooper." <u>Baseball Reference</u>. Gracenote: A Nielsen Company. Sports Reference LLC. Copyright 2000-2018; "Mort Cooper." <u>Baseball Almanac</u>. Baseball Almanac, Inc. Copyright 2000-2018; "Mort Cooper Stats." <u>Statmuse</u>. <u>www.statmuse.com</u>; and Neuman, Jeffrey and John Warner Davenport. <u>The Cardinals</u>. New York: Macmillan Publishing Company, Inc., 1983.

Illustration by Carissa McDonald.

Postscript

In April of 2019, the St. Louis Cardinals announced that Mort Cooper had been selected by a Red Ribbon Committee to be inducted into the St. Louis Cardinals Hall of Fame. Cooper will be enshrined in the Hall in August of 2019 along with former Cardinal standouts Jason Isringhausen and Scott Rolen.

Members of the St. Louis Cardinals Hall of Fame

Class of 2019:

Mort Cooper
Scott Rolen
Jason Isringhausen

List below is in alphabetical order:

Jim Bottomley	Ray Lankford
Ken Boyer	Tony LaRussa
Sam Breadon	Marty Marion
Harry Brecheen	Pepper Martin
Lou Brock	Tim McCarver
Jack Buck	Willie McGee
August A. Busch, Jr.	Mark McGwire
Chris Carpenter	Joe Medwick
Vince Coleman	Johnny Mize
Dizzy Dean	Terry Moore
Jim Edmonds	Stan Musial
Curt Flood	Branch Rickey
Bob Forsch	Red Schoendienst
Frankie Frisch	Mike Shannon
Bob Gibson	Ted Simmons
Chick Hafey	Enos Slaughter
Jesse Haines	Ozzie Smith
Whitey Herzog	Billy Southworth
Rogers Hornsby	Bruce Sutter
George Kissell	Joe Torre

Acknowledgements

I would like to express my sincere thanks to the following people. Without their help and guidance this book would not have been possible.

Thanks to Danielle Pucci of the Boston Public Library who put me in contact with Bob Cullum, grandson of Leslie Jones. Mr. Cullum graciously allowed me to use three photos from his grandfather's extensive and historic photographic collection housed at the Boston Public Library. Anyone who enjoys brilliant photographic artistry should peruse the Leslie Jones Collection at Boston Public.

Also special thanks to Megan Spainhour, Digital Imaging Specialist at the Tennessee State Library and Archives. She was a great help in obtaining permission to use a photograph from the collection titled "Johnny Beazley and Baseball in Tennessee."

Special thanks to Carissa McDonald who contributed several beautiful illustrations for the book. Her photographic and artistic portfolio may be viewed at carissamcd.wixsite.com/photography.

Finally, thanks to my wife Lori who always provides sound guidance and editorial assistance. You are the love of my life.

As always any mistakes in fact or conclusion are all my own.

About the Author: Michael Murphy is a retired educator from Missouri who taught for over twenty-five years in Missouri's public schools and colleges. He holds a Bachelor of Arts degree from Murray State University and a Master's from the University of Mississippi. He is the author of *Elsie's Story: This Story Has No Hero.* His work has also been published in *Instructor, Poet Forum, Good Old Days Magazine,* and the *Annual Conference of the Missouri National Guard Association.*

Made in the USA
Monee, IL
28 April 2022

95556177R00033